73

WAYS

TO HELP

YOUR BABY

*SLEEP

Stewart, Tabori & Chang
New York

"Be glad and honored that your baby needs you so much. He is probably the only person in the world who will love you 100 percent without criticism or reservation. Enjoy his company... Make him feel good and let him make you feel good, too."

— **Penelope Leach,** *Your Baby & Child*

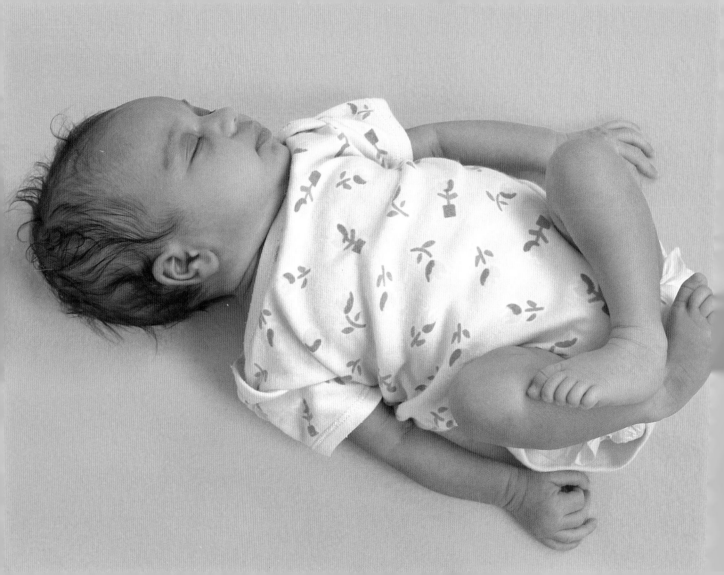

foreword

New parents often spend months preparing for the arrival of their baby. They paint and decorate the nursery, buy a crib, and receive adorable clothes from friends and family. They read up on feeding and decide on breast or bottle. They know what number to call if the baby is sick. But, no matter how prepared or knowledgeable they may be, new parents are almost always surprised at how little sleep they get. Even new parents who are pediatricians are surprised, and like other parents, they are tired.

Let's face it: Taking care of a newborn is exhausting all by itself—there are diapers (and more diapers), around-the-clock feeding, changes of clothes (yours and the baby's), laundry, constant wariness that something could be wrong, and so on.

Throw into the mix the fact that new parents rarely sleep more than a few hours in a row, and being the parent of a newborn becomes the most challenging job in the world. Not only that, but at the one-week visit, infants are often sound asleep, and their parents sheepishly reveal that she doesn't sleep at night. Of course, most pediatricians reply, her days and nights are confused. Give it time!

There is good news and bad news about babies and sleep. The good news is that there are absolutely ways to help your baby to fall asleep, and stay asleep at night. The bad news is that it can take some effort on your part. Life is definitely different with a baby in the home.

For starters, you might have to adjust your expectations. During the first six weeks of her life, a newborn rarely sleeps more than three or four hours in a row at night. Twins are often on different schedules from one another, and preemies can be completely unpredictable. At twelve weeks, periods of nighttime sleep may extend up to six—or even eight—consecutive hours, and by six months, your baby is capable of ten to twelve hours of nighttime sleep.

I've seen plenty of new mothers who tell me that they honestly don't believe their little ones will ever sleep through the night. (That includes the author of this book.) A nurse friend of mine once told me—confessed is more like it—that when her firstborn was sleeping in his crib in the master bedroom, she found that she was waking up constantly and checking on him. She and her physician husband had to make the decision to move their newborn to his own room because she was actually disturbing the baby's sleep, her husband's sleep, and her own sleep.

The shelves of your local bookstore are lined with in-depth descriptions of how babies sleep and how to get them to sleep better and longer. This book brings together the suggestions of many experts, but presents them through the eyes of a young mother who has tried all of them. You can pick and choose, giving each tip the time to make a difference. Sometimes it takes up to two weeks for a method to succeed. Sometimes it doesn't work. Sometimes your baby will figure it out herself. Other times, you may have to endure some tears. From my experience taking care of infants and children for more than thirty years, there is no single sure-fire way to make your infant sleep. You will need to find the way that works for you and your family. Here are 73—at least one of them is sure to be useful!

Marianne E. Felice, MD
Professor and Chair, Department of Pediatrics,
University of Massachusetts Medical School
Physician-in-Chief, UMass Memorial Children's Medical Center

introduction

When my brother heard that I was writing this book, he laughed. My daughter was a terrible sleeper as an infant. For that matter, so was my son. But I learned plenty during those sleepless nights of nursing, rocking, and (me) crying. Mostly I figured out that while there was little I could actually do to *make* my newborn babies sleep, there was lots I could do to help them (and again, me) to relax. They soon grew into the good little sleepers they are today. After I began getting some shut-eye myself, I was able to count the methods. Turns out there really are 73.

Some of my suggestions are more for you than for your baby. Being a new parent is hard. Part of the challenge is letting your baby be a baby. If she wakes up every hour, she isn't trying to torture you. And you're not a terrible person for getting frustrated.

The ideas you'll find here can help your growing baby sleep longer and better. They will definitely help you to feel useful in the uncharted and ever-changing landscape of parenthood. Knowing what REM sleep means is useful for someone, I'm sure, but the charts and graphs in most baby sleep books were completely incomprehensible to me as a new mother. I preferred staring at the sleeping babies gracing the book jackets as I nursed my girl for the tenth time in twenty-four hours. When she slept, I couldn't pull my eyes away from her. The sweetness of my babies asleep would always erase all my anxieties of the moment, which is why I wanted photographs in my book.

Your baby will sleep through the night eventually, and although I know from experience that you will find this literally impossible to fathom, you will miss the feeling of a soft baby against your cheek at 3:00 a.m. Trust me.

And my brother's baby? Champion sleeper. He's a master of "the ways."

keep in mind

Be Realistic

Newborns are not meant to sleep through the night. As your baby grows and becomes more attuned to the world around him, he will gain the ability to sleep for longer periods of time and to differentiate between night and day.

During the early newborn days, when your baby's sleep is topsy-turvy—usually until he's about twelve weeks old—you should do everything you can to comfort him. Let him sleep in the swing, the bouncy seat, in a swaddle or a sling. Feed him when he's hungry. Comfort him when he's crying. Make sure he's dry and comfortable. Try to start a bedtime routine, but keep it simple: Clean, change, feed, bed, same routine every night.

Once he's getting more predictable, from about three months to six months, he'll be more aware of the world. He'll smile at you, reach for things, maybe even roll over and try to sleep on his belly. At this point, you'll want to keep up the routine and try to phase out some of your most desperate measures, like driving with him until he falls asleep.

By the time he's six months old, your baby may be sitting up and laughing. You are starting to feed him solid foods. He's much more predictable and no longer needs to eat during his nighttime sleep. Now you might practice one of the more structured "sleep training" techniques listed at the end of the book. Please try not to leave your baby to cry before he is at least four months old, if not six months—and "crying it out" rarely works without a routine already in place.

Trust Your Instincts

You're still going to want to read the essential tomes on sleep. But don't take every suggestion to heart and judge yourself. There's no one "right" way. If you read ten books on babies and sleep, you'll find ten conflicting messages: Let the baby cry, don't let the baby cry, nurse the baby to sleep, always put the baby to bed awake, shorten naps, increase naps, and so on. They can all work. You just have to pay attention to your little one and find the method that best suits your family.

The odds are excellent that you are not going to permanently screw up your baby's sleep habits before he's out of diapers. Check with the pediatrician when concerns come up, and try to give whatever sleep methods you choose time to work—at least one week; better, two weeks.

When You're Overwhelmed

Every new parent feels really, really stressed at times, but if your anxieties are getting the better of you, tell someone. Your obstetrician can help you with coping skills and, if necessary, medication. It's not a sign of weakness to be overwhelmed and even unhappy during this "special time"—every person reacts differently to the hormonal ups-and-downs, lack of sleep, and general emotional turmoil brought on by a new baby. Be nice to yourself and ask for help when you need it.

1

Food, Glorious Food

Don't underestimate the sleep-inducing effect of food. Babies only eat when they are hungry, so always consider this when he's not sleeping for you. If he's rooting for something to suck on, and a pacifier or finger only frustrates him, he wants the real thing.

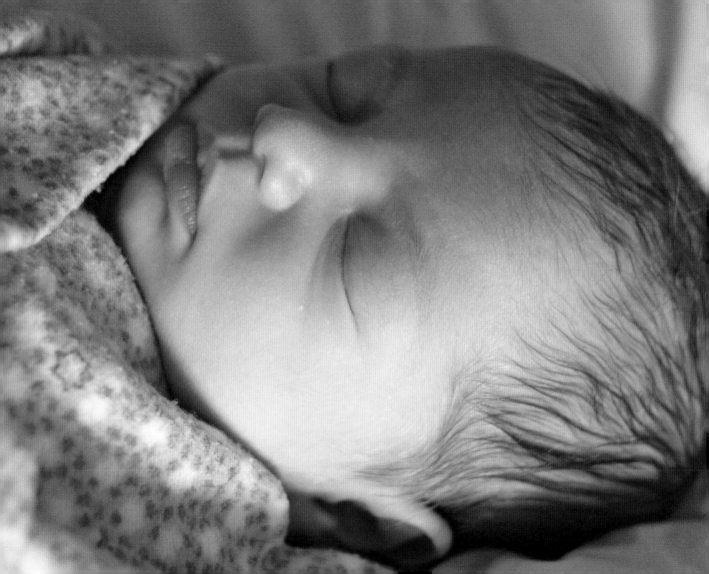

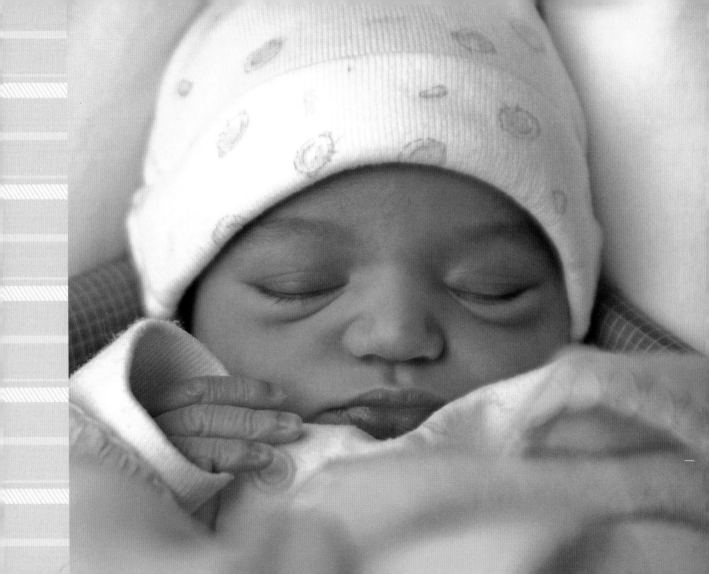

Bedtime for Baby

For the first six weeks of your baby's life, let go of the idea of strict schedules. This can actually be relaxing and help you sleep: You'll have to catch forty winks whenever she's asleep. Baby's nighttime "bedtime" should be around 10:00 p.m.; you'll want to feed and change her if she's wet but after this time, try to keep your interactions with her very low-key until the sun rises. It's a case of adjusting your expectations—newborns need to eat every two to three hours at this age.

Swaddle Him with Love

Swaddling infants has been common practice around the world for thousands of years, and it's a familiar sight at hospitals. Wrapping your baby snugly comforts him (as if you were holding him tight, or even as if he were still in the womb) and immobilizing his arms prevents the startling reflex that tends to wake babies. Lucky for uncoordinated parents, you can now buy swaddling blankets made with simple velcro flaps—some come complete with a blanket bottom to keep baby cozy.

3

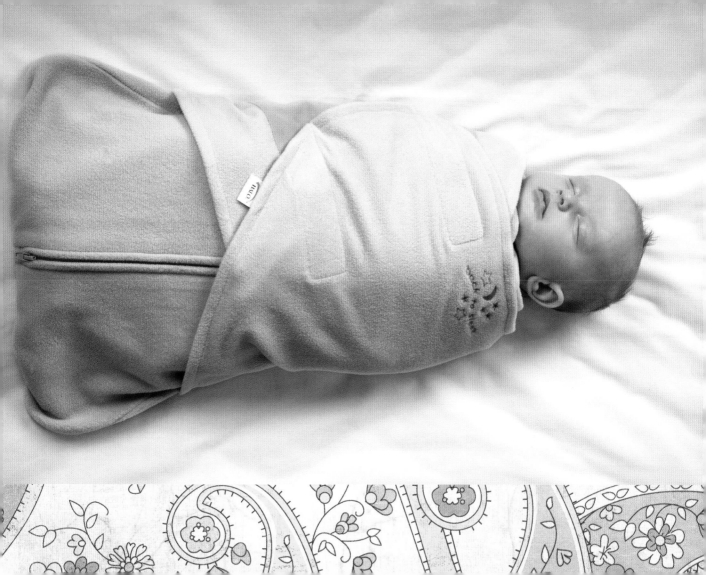

Location, Location

Pediatricians recommend that your baby sleep in your room for the first month or two of his life. After that time, though, reconsider the real estate in your home. It's impossible to ignore your baby's cry, but consider this: You might actually be interrupting your *baby's* sleep by checking on him so often.

4

Fools Rush In

Your baby makes noises while he's sleeping.
Let him sniff and sigh and gurgle and maybe
even cry out before you reach for him—
sometimes he just needs to settle down. If
you wait five minutes, you might be surprised.

5

Stay Close but Not Together

The faster you can respond to your baby in the middle of the night, the less likely either of you are to wake fully. Rather than keeping her in your bed, though, where the dangers far outweigh the benefits, consider a co-sleeper, a crib that opens on to the side of your bed so you can reach out to soothe your baby without rising.

Loving Sleep

7

New parents love sleep; even if you weren't a big sleeper before you had a baby, you probably value it now more than ever. When you're putting baby down, remind him of the wonderful night he has ahead of him, dreaming his wonderful dreams. You're not banishing him to bed, you're sending him to lovely la-la land.

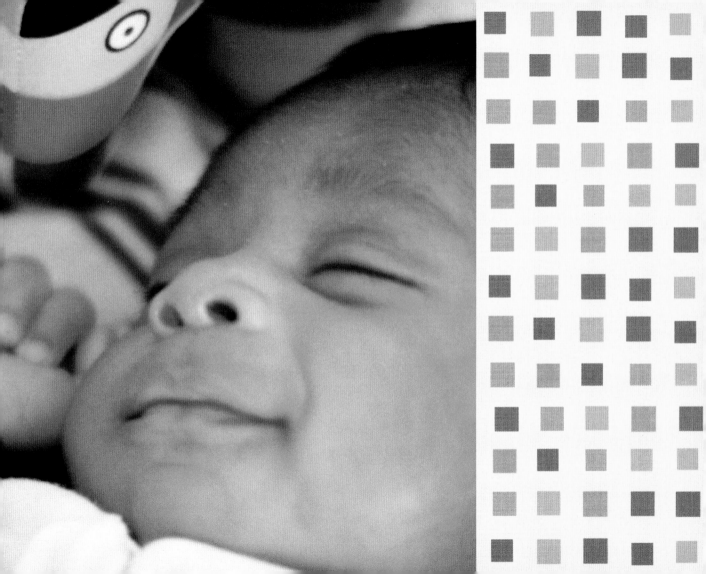

The Big House

8

A crib can seem awfully big to a little baby. For the first few months, you might be better off with a bassinet or special sleeping basket. Do try to get her used to a crib, though; believe it or not, she'll someday outgrow even that. Try putting the basket inside the crib, or placing tightly rolled towels along the crib's sides—or co-sleeper, if you're using one—to make it cozier.

Share the Joy

If possible, you and your partner should make a plan for middle-of-the-night care. For example, some couples break the night into two shifts; others plan mom for one or two breastfeeding breaks and leave the rest up to the non-lactating part of the team. Whatever you decide, discuss it *before* it's 2 a.m. and you're both cranky.

10

Don't Keep Score

If you're reading this book, you're probably the parent who is doing most of the nighttime caretaking. It's difficult not to be resentful of your partner—or even your baby—but try to let that go. Either ask for more help or remind yourself that this time is precious. Because it is.

11

Back to Sleep

A baby is almost always soothed by being on her side or tummy, yet research has proven that it's safer for babies to sleep on their backs. Try swaying her to sleep on her side, in a swaddle to make her feel secure, then gently roll her onto her back into bed. Once she can roll over, though, it's baby's choice.

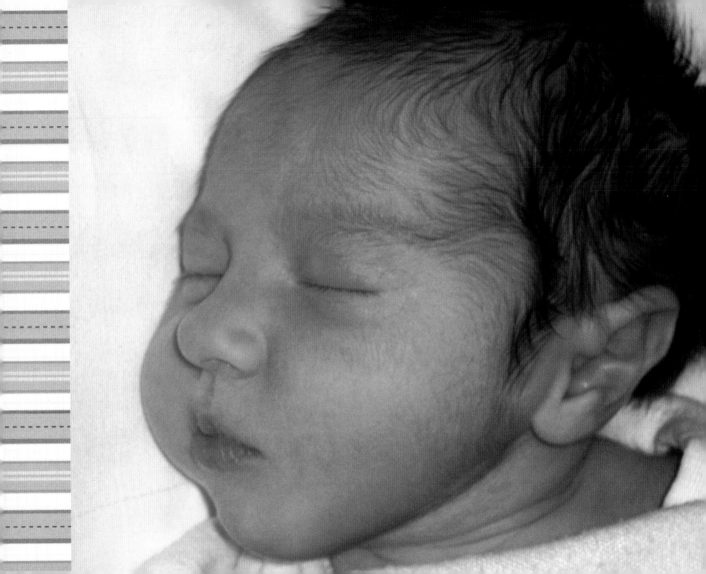

He Was Such a Sleeper!

Don't despair if your round-the-clock sleeper suddenly becomes a night owl when you leave the hospital. This is absolutely normal, although it's sure to come as a shock. Just go with the flow—the pendulum will swing again once he's a teenager.

12

13

Dim the Lights

Some babies like to sleep in complete darkness, mimicking the womb. Others like low lights. In any case, you'll need to see for nighttime visits, so it's worth thinking about putting a dimmer switch into the nursery. Or use a nightlight with a switch that you can turn on and off.

Warm the Bed

There's nothing as pleasant as slipping into warm sheets, and your baby would agree. Before baby goes down, warm her bed with a hot water bottle. (Never leave it in the crib, however.) Or try putting her blanket in the dryer for a few minutes. Always make sure that there are no hot spots. You may find yourself using the same trick!

14

Expectations, Baby

The idea of creating a bedtime routine when you first return from the hospital might seem crazy, but it's worth the trouble. Start simple: Bath, story, milk, and a song is a fine routine and sets the groundwork for good sleep as baby grows.

15

16

Good Night, Every Night

You might not want to read the same book every night, but a baby likes to know what to expect. Get a copy of *Good Night Moon* and add your own variations, saying good night to each part of your baby's room before she peacefully dozes off to sleep.

17

Knead to Sleep

Who doesn't love a nice massage after a bath? Lie your baby down on a soft towel on his changing table or the floor. Warm unscented massage oil between your hands and gently stroke his skin with your fingers, from his toes up to his belly. Then gently on across his chest and down his arms to his tiny fingers. Shift him on his side to stroke his back. Finish with a gentle sweep over his forehead and ears. Keep a towel or blanket draped over the parts you're not touching so he stays toasty warm.

18

Wrap Her Up

Swaddling is wonderful, but forget about trying to use those tiny receiving blankets from the hospital. You'll only get frustrated. Instead, buy a large, square blanket, ideally 42" x 42", made of a material with some give, such as cotton or fleece. You will doubtless worry that this is a cruel trick (straightjacket, anyone?), but when you see how calm it makes your baby, you'll be a convert.

Love Your Lovey

19

A blanket or special toy can help babies transition from caregiver to bed. Sometimes a baby will find his own lovey, and you should encourage this. Or pick an object to give to him while he nurses, rides in the car, rests in bed, or does other quiet activities. If you like, sleep with it yourself so it has your smell on it. And once your baby is old enough to roll over and snuggle with his soft doggy or fuzzy blanket, leave him be!

Mommy Lies

When you hear a mommy brag that her two-week-old is sleeping through the night already, don't forget that she's probably exaggerating. In fact, most experienced mothers (and pediatricians) would be worried if a two-week-old slept through the night. This won't be the first time you'll be tempted to compare your child to someone else's. Don't tune into it.

20

Hollywood Mama

21

Make sure you get yourself out of the house every day. Tiny babies are pretty portable—and movie matinees can be just the ticket when the weather is extreme. Some cinemas even feature "mommy matinees" during off-times. Nursing in a cool theater during a hot summer day is a lovely treat—your baby is certain to snooze in your arms.

Nature's Nightcap

The hormones in breast milk help make baby sleepy—and a good feeding also helps mom to doze off for an all-important rest .

22

23

You Feed What You Eat

As if new motherhood isn't difficult enough, breast-feeding moms worry that their baby is fussy because of something they ate. No real evidence of this exists, but if you are concerned, cut out coffee, tea, sodas, and chocolate for a few weeks to see if it helps. (Why don't they make decaffeinated chocolate…?)

Mo' Better Milk

Lots of new moms feed their babies every hour or so between 5:00 p.m. and bedtime. Then it's nighty-night, hopefully until the wee hours.

Tank 'Em Up

Give your baby her last nursing or bottle just as you're going to bed, even if she's already down. Without waking her up completely, brush her mouth with the nipple and she's sure to latch on for a late night snack that could give you an extra hour or two of snooze time.

25

So Noisy

Believe it or not, your baby is used to lots and lots of loud sounds—the sound of your organs working right next to baby's ears made for some terrific background noise. A white noise machine, or even the radio set to static, can do a remarkable job of calming your future *Spinal Tap* fan. Just don't forget to turn it to "11."

26

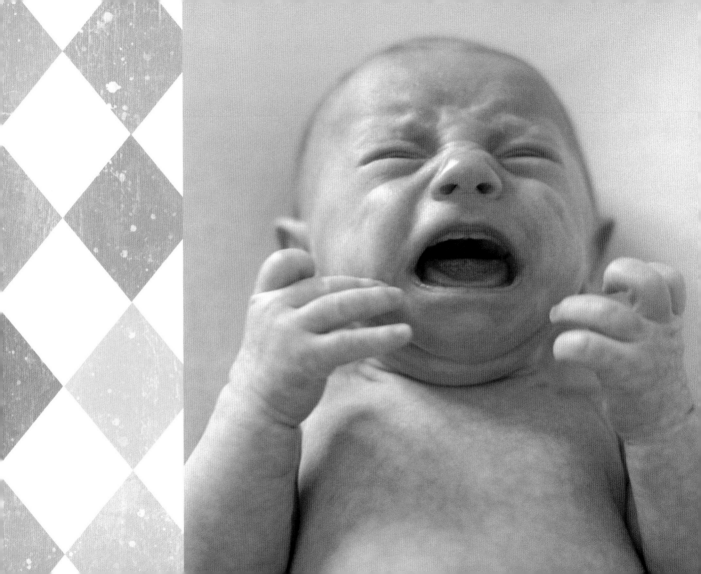

Stay Up, Sleep Better?

Trying to keep your baby up late so that he'll sleep better at night will surely backfire. An overtired baby will resist sleep more than a rested one, so keep naps regular and bedtime early. After the first few months, most babies should go to bed between 7:00 and 8:00. Give it a whirl.

27

Counter-Intuitive Bedtime Trick

Believe it or not, if your baby is having trouble falling asleep, he may need an earlier bedtime. Try moving it up 15 minutes or so and see what happens. Some babies sleep from 6:00 to 6:00. (Many others do not.)

28

29

Color Her Sleepy

Remember when feng shui was all the rage? Sleep deprivation will make you a believer again: Try painting baby's room a relaxing blue or lavender, and choose bedding in a monochromatic scheme to match.

30

Whoosh, Whoosh

Lean over the crib and half-sing, half-chant "whoosh, whoosh" over and over. Think of ocean waves as you're doing it. Hopefully baby will grow as snoozy as you do sitting on a beach in the sun, listening to the sea.

Old - Tyme Rockin'

If you can find one, an old-fashioned cradle that rocks can do wonders the first few weeks of baby's life. Gentle rocking can help her doze off to sleep, and if she startles, another gentle rock can keep her there.

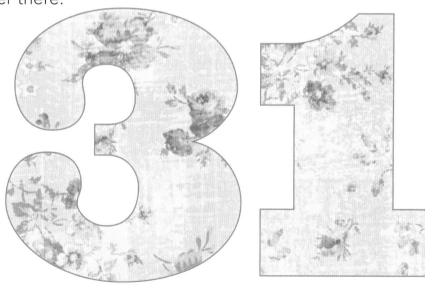

32

Tell Him a Secret

Make up a good-night wish for your baby, and whisper it in his ear each time he goes to sleep. Don't tell anyone else what you say.

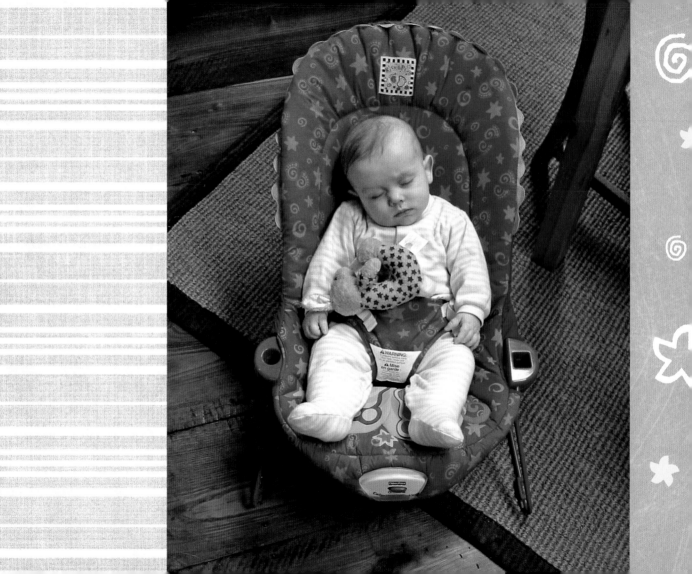

Baby-Matic

Otherwise known as the swing, although a vibrating bouncy seat will also do the trick, this device will make your baby very happy and calm—especially if you throw in a swaddle—which makes you happy and calm, too. Once he's out, turn off the motor to allow your baby to fall into a very deep sleep. This is best for the early months, for daytime sleep.

34

Play in the Day

When you feed your baby in the daytime, play a little peek-a-boo or sing a song to remind him that it's time to be awake. Don't force the issue if he's a real sleepy-head at first, but be aware of making daytime, playtime.

Pacifiers Pacifying

The age-old debate about using pacifiers got a positive boost when the American Academy of Pediatrics recommended using a pacifier to help young babies to fall asleep; early studies show that it seems to help prevent SIDS. This is most important between two and six months of age. (After this time, pacifiers can increase the number of ear infections, so that's something to keep in mind.) If your baby likes the "binky" and it helps her sleep, by all means—use that sucker!

35

Carry On

Try using a sling or carrier to keep baby close to you and your heart. She'll probably fall asleep and you can tend to yourself while she's so peaceful. After her early newborn days, try putting her in her own bed after she's asleep so she'll get used to being there.

36

Eat Enough Each Time

Your baby needs to nurse for at least twelve to fifteen minutes per breast to get a well-rounded meal.
The rich "cream" comes at the end of the feeding, and that's what will fuel him for good sleep.

37

38

Wake a Sleeping Baby?

Some experts say never wake a sleeping baby, while others suggest waking him for milk every three hours around the clock. Waking your baby at night won't benefit anyone. Instead, encourage your baby to eat more during the day and early evening. Break up a daytime nap that is three or four hours long with a feeding; at night, however, let him sleep to his heart's content.

39

Fresh Air

Your mother said it, and her mother probably
said it before her, but it's just true. Fresh air will
do a body (and a baby) good. A rest on the
beach is always a treat.

Bundle Up

If your fussy boy is getting cabin fever, bundle him in fleece and take him for a walk. If he falls asleep, roll the stroller into the house and grab yourself a nap on the couch.

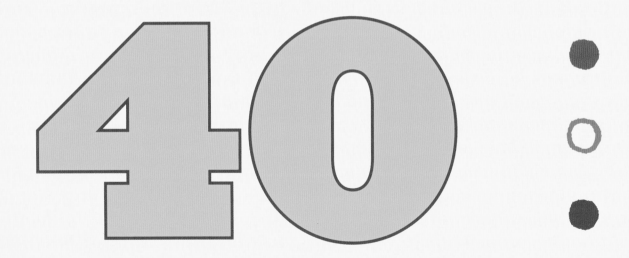

40

Take a Ride

If the only way your precious one will take a snooze is in the back of the car, go out and take a ride. Once he's asleep, though, stop the car and either put your own seat back for a rest or carry in baby, car seat and all. This is best for younger babies, after the first few months, try not to rely on this trick.

A Calm Parent is a Good Parent

Your baby can sense your emotions. When you're upset, she becomes agitated. When you're calm, she becomes calmer. Practice relaxing your muscles *before* you pick her up. Let your eyes soften, your jaw get slack. Check your shoulders—are they raised? Let them go. Now pick up baby and don't worry that she's crying her little heart out. This too will pass.

The Language of Babes

Recent feeding? Check. Dry diaper? Check. Crying doesn't always mean hunger, but how do you know what your baby needs? Watching the clock can help. If your baby is dry and full, and has been awake more than two hours, she might actually be sleepy.

No Time for Chatting

Nighttime feedings should be short and sweet. Keep the lights low and the cuddling to a minimum. You can "shush" but now isn't the time to comment on cute toes. If this sounds unkind to you, remember how much happier you'll be in the morning—how much more loving and emotionally available you'll be—when you're both sleeping through the night.

44

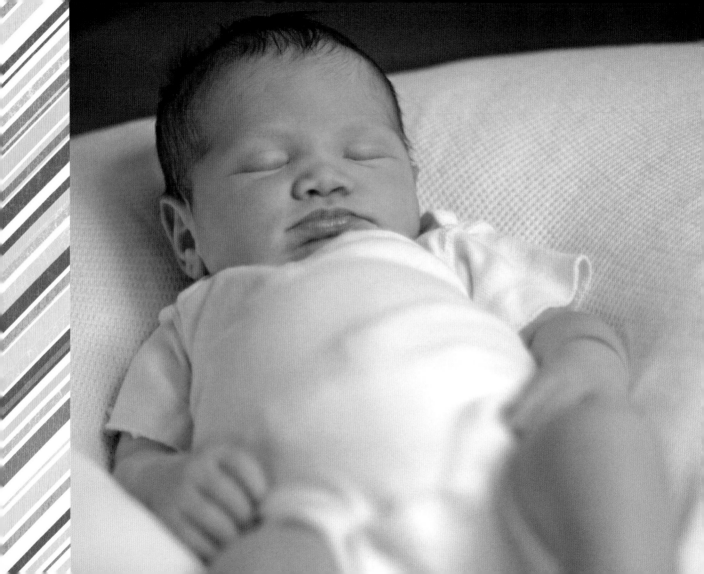

45

Diaper Do's and Don'ts

If your little one tends to get soaked through during the night, try special overnight diapers, or something called "diaper doublers," and slather the diaper cream on to her dried bottom. You really don't need to change her unless she has a poop—today's diapers are amazingly efficient at keeping baby from feeling wet even if the diaper is full.

Hold On

Hold your baby with his head draped over your shoulder and his belly against your upper chest when he seems fussy. Rubbing his back while he's in this position will soothe him and help him to burp. And if you're very still, you can even feel his heart beating against you.

47

Tame the Tummy

If your baby spits up a lot after feeding, and seems uncomfortable lying down, try tilting his crib with phone books under its legs, keeping his head up. Or buy special wedges to put under his mattress to keep his head higher than his feet.

The Two-Hour Rule

For the first four months, try to put your baby down for a rest after two hours of active time. That means if she's awake at 6:30, aim for a nap at 8:30. Even if she doesn't seem tired, what do you have to lose?

48

49

Twenty to Go

It typically takes a baby about twenty minutes to go from wake to sleep. Give him a chance to get there before you give up.

50

Same Time, Same Place

Babies love routine—and routine is the best way to teach them that light means playtime and dark means sleepy time. A kiss from big sister is a favorite way to end the day.

51

Good Mommy

Try not to blame yourself for your baby's sleeplessness. It doesn't mean you're a bad parent. Remind yourself of this, and remind your friends and family to remind you, too.

52

Natural Rhythms

Keeping a log of your baby's sleep patterns—even if you don't think there's a pattern to be found—can prove helpful. You might discover more of a rhythm than you think exists, which in turn, can help you know when your baby naturally feels sleepy or awake.

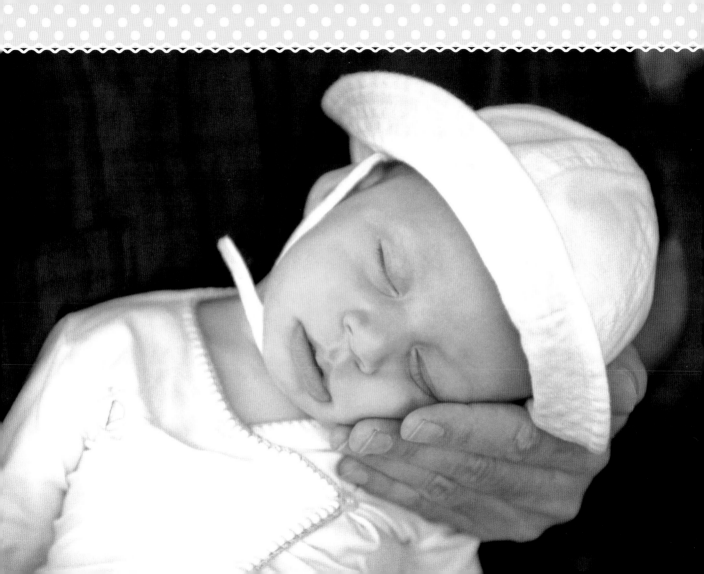

Three Days / Seven Days

The old wives' tale is three days to make a habit, seven days to break it. So if you consistently miss your baby's bedtime routine, try to commit to a stretch of doing the same thing every night for at least three days. Don't mix it up—remember, familiarity equals expectation equals sleep. Or something like that.

53

Big Yawn

Like adults, babies yawn when they are sleepy. It may be catching—start that bedtime routine pronto.

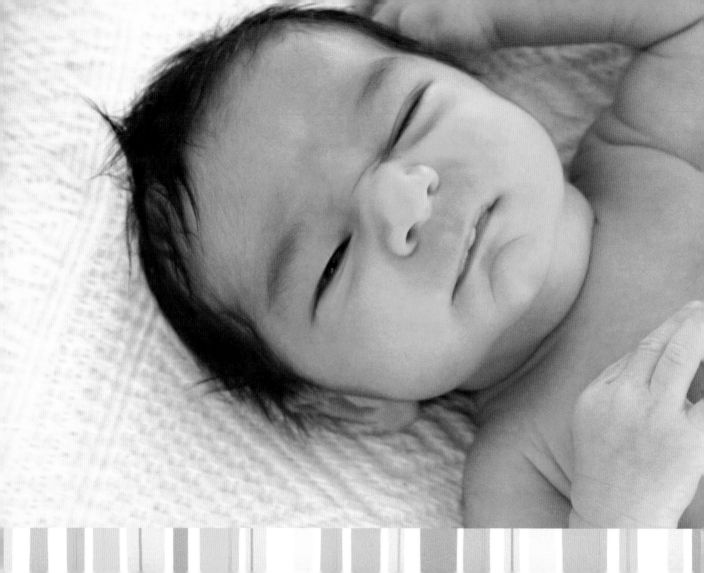

Common Scents

Use an essential oil—lavender is nice—in a diffuser, or on a tissue, in your baby's room. Bring it with you when you travel and the new place will smell just like home.

Try a Bottle

Do formula-fed babies sleep more? This doesn't appear to be the case, but allowing someone else to feed your baby once a day can provide you with a break. You can sleep a longer shift if you choose the nighttime feed for the bottle. If you're breast feeding and it's going well, pump milk for the feeding without worrying about diminishing your supply.

56

57

Solid Myth

Many a mother is told that the sooner she feeds her baby solid foods, the sooner her baby will sleep through the night. There is nothing to prove this; in fact, for the first six months of their lives, babies should be receiving all the nutrition they need from breast milk or formula. You can feed your baby more frequently during the day if you think she's truly hungry in the middle of the night—but never add cereal to a bottle. If your pediatrician agrees, you can start with rice cereal at four months, using a spoon and propping baby upright in a high chair.

58

Pay Attention

A baby who isn't interested in eating might be ready for bed. Put him down before he starts to fuss. (Or falls asleep in his high chair!)

59

P.J. Time

Change baby into a soft sleeper at night as another signal that it's bedtime. Buy four or five of the same type to reinforce the idea, and don't use them for anything else.

Good Morning, Sunshine

Don't forget a morning routine, too. Open the shades, let the sun in, and sing good morning. Remind her it's time to wake up and play.

60

61

Eat Enough, Sleep Enough

By the time a baby is twelve weeks old, he should be able to go at least six hours without eating. But how do you know he's getting enough food? Besides the most obvious—he's growing!—the rule of thumb for a 24-hour day is three ounces for each pound your baby weighs. So an eight-pound baby needs about 24 ounces of milk.

Phasing Out Crutches

When your baby is growing more "settled," at about three or four months, start phasing out some of the crutches you may have used in those first crazy weeks at home. The walking, driving, 24/7 nursing, and other last-ditch efforts don't need to be stopped cold turkey, but you probably should begin to help baby help himself get to sleep. The best way to do this is to start with your method, but try to put your baby down *before* he is in a very deep sleep. You can pick him up again if he cries, but every day try to let him do a little bit more for himself. Don't forget that you're coaching him how to sleep, a skill that will last forever.

62

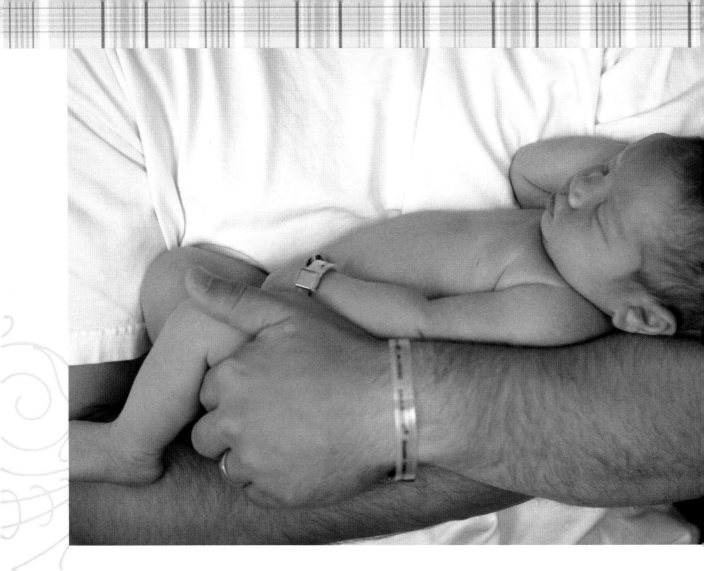

Experience is Key

If your baby can easily fall asleep in your arms or on your breast, he has no real problem getting to sleep; he's just gotten used to falling asleep in your presence. Your job will be to help him gain experience falling asleep in his crib.

63

Snug as a Bug

Zip baby up in a wearable blanket, or "sack," and she will stay toasty all night. You can also do midnight changes more easily if need be, carrying your warm bundle out of bed and unzipping from the bottom for a quick diaper change.

64

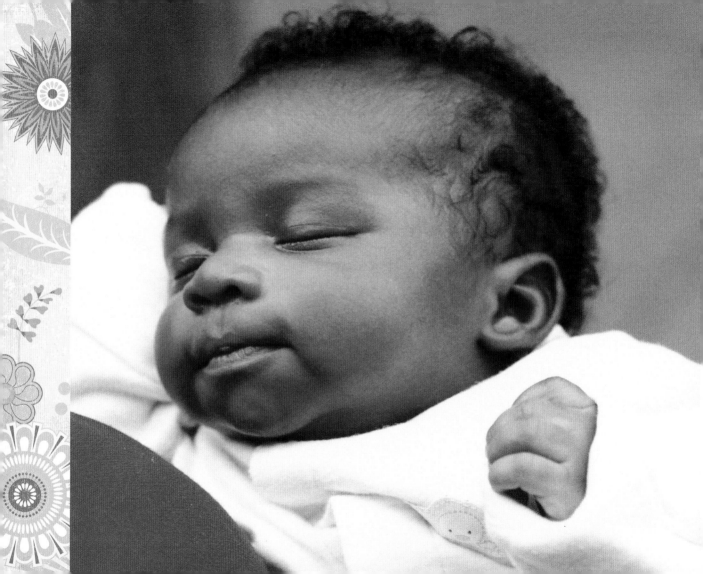

65

Sleep How You Wake

A baby who is rocked to sleep every night in her daddy's arms, then moved to her crib after she's fast asleep, might well have problems falling back to sleep herself after a normal waking in the night. If this is the case, make sure she falls asleep in the same place she'll wake up. That means putting her down *before* she's fully asleep, in her crib. This becomes more critical after she's twelve weeks old.

66

Numbers Game

You've been keeping track of his sleep, and you discover that your baby has in fact gone more than six or seven hours without eating—bingo, you're ready to make that stretch happen during your sleeping time.

Sleep Training 101

If you've decided to make a concerted effort to try to get your four-month-old to sleep more hours at night, undertake the first days of this mission when you can most afford lost sleep yourself. A long weekend is better than the day before a big presentation at work.

67

68

Nursing to Sleep?

Nursing your baby to sleep is such a wonderful way to end the day—who would want to stop that? No mom I know. However, if your baby is still waking more than once in the night after he's three or four months old and cannot get back to sleep without nursing, you might want to try rousing him a bit after feeding him at bedtime, so that he's awake when you put him in his crib. Or, tweak his schedule so that you nurse him in another room and follow the feeding with a bath or massage.

To Cry or Not to Cry

"Sleep training" is often seen as a nice way of saying, "crying it out." But letting your baby cry until she falls asleep is not a method unto itself. A good sleep routine should already be in place before you consider letting your baby cry—and most pediatricians agree that this tends to work best with a baby who is at least six months old, although you can try it when she's four months old if you're desperate. If you decide this is the way to go, make sure you return to baby's room every five to ten minutes (you can stretch out this interval each time) to reassure her with a pat that you're there, you love her, and she can do this.

69

70

Find a Good Listener

If you're struggling to put together a bedtime routine, and your baby just doesn't seem to be catching on to the plan, set up a time every morning to talk to someone who you trust and who understands babies. Maybe it's your mom, maybe it's your partner; recounting what has happened the night before can put it in perspective and keep you from utter despair.

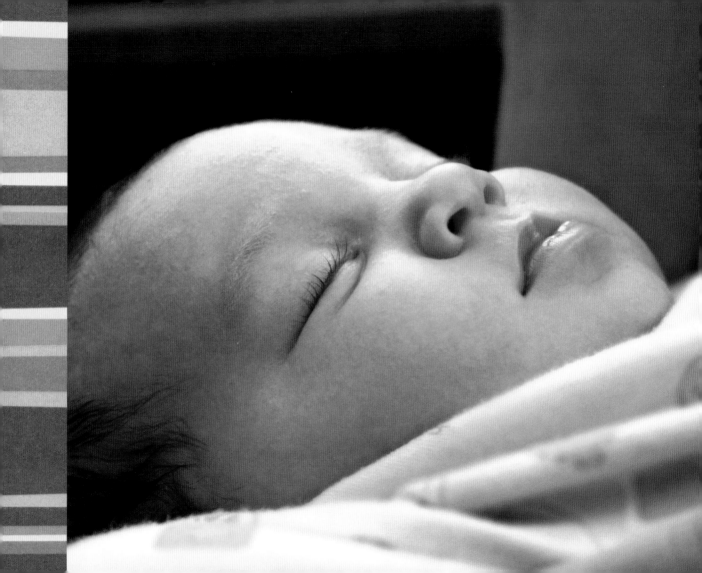

Sleep Coach

A coach can't get into a game and play for his team any more than you can crawl into your baby's crib and sleep for your little one. You can comfort with pats and encouraging words, but at the end of the day, she needs to learn to fall asleep by herself.

71

72

Call in the Troops

If your baby is six months old and still waking in the night for food, you should probably wean him off eating in the wee hours. It's very hard for a breast-feeding mother to refuse her crying baby a nip at night, so start with a bottle of breast milk or formula given by someone else. That alone might be boring enough to stop baby from waking up. If not, dilute the bottle with water each day for a week. By the end, your baby will probably decide it's not worth rising for some lukewarm water.

Love Outlasts Everything

Despite your best intentions—you have the schedule, he's in the crib, the stars are aligned—if your baby has to shed some tears on his journey to learning how to sleep, you should rest assured that it won't be a traumatic experience, resulting in psychological damage. In fact, he'll rise in the morning happy as can be, ready for your love and attention.

73

resources

Brazelton, T. Berry and Joshua D. Sparrow. *Sleep, the Brazelton Way*. New York, NY: Perseus Books, 2003.

Casarjian, Bethany E. and Diane H. Dillon. *Mommy Mantras*. New York, NY: Broadway Books, 2006.

Douglas, Ann. *Sleep Solutions for Your Baby, Toddler and Preschooler*. Hoboken, NJ: Wiley, 2006.

Ferber, Richard. *Solve Your Child's Sleep Problems*. New York, NY: Simon & Schuster, 2006.

Hogg, Tracy. *Secrets of the Baby Whisperer*. New York, NY: Ballantine, 2002.

Holland, Katy. *Johnson's Sleep*. New York, NY: DK Publishing, 2006.

Kabat - Zin, Jon and Myla. *Everyday Blessings: The Inner Work of Mindful Parenting*. New York, NY: Hyperion, 1998.

Karp, Harvey. *The Happiest Baby on the Block*. New York, NY: Bantam, 2002.

Leach, Penelope. *Your Baby & Child*. New York, NY: Knopf, 1997.

Mindell, Jodi A. *Sleeping Through the Night*. New York, NY: HarperCollins, 2005.

Pantley, Elizabeth. *The No-Cry Sleep Solution*. New York, NY: McGraw-Hill, 2002.

Weissbluth, Marc. *Healthy Sleep Habits, Happy Child*. New York, NY: Ballantine, 1999.

West, Kim. *Good Night, Sleep Tight*. New York, NY: CDS Books, 2005.

www.aap.org (American Academy of Pediatrics, has most current information on sleep standards)

www.babycenter.com (Has helpful comparisons of different methods; also, parent forums)

www.sleepnet.com

acknowledgments

LeAnna Weller Smith designed the most beautiful book imaginable. A big thank you to you, LeAnna, and to my collaborator, Dr. Marianne Felice. Also, buckets of gratitude to Leslie Stoker, Marisa Bulzone, Kristen Latta, Ann Stratton, Larry Dorfman, and everyone at Stewart, Tabori & Chang. To my mom and dad, who have always given me great advice, and far more than 73 pieces of it. I'm so happy to be your daughter. With lots of love and thanks to all my family, particularly Owen, Susie, and Bryant.

Published in 2007 by Stewart, Tabori & Chang
An imprint of Harry N. Abrams, Inc.

Text copyright © 2007 by Ann Treistman
Foreword copyright © 2007 by Marianne E. Felice, MD

Library of Congress Cataloging-in-Publication Data

Treistman, Ann.
 73 ways to help your baby sleep / by Ann Treistman ; foreword by Marianne E. Felice.
    p. cm.
 Includes bibliographical references.
 ISBN-13: 978-1-58479-625-1
 ISBN-10: 1-58479-625-1
 1. Infants--Sleep--Popular works. I. Title. II. Title: Seventy-three ways to help your baby sleep.

RJ506.S55T74 2007
649'.122--dc22

2006037122

Editors: Marisa Bulzone and Kristen Latta
Designer: LeAnna Weller Smith
Production Manager: Jacquie Poirier

The text of this book was composed in Avenir, Century Schoolbook, and Wendy LP.

Printed and bound in China.
10 9 8 7 6 5 4 3 2 1

HNA
harry n. abrams, inc.
a subsidiary of La Martinière Groupe

115 West 18th Street
New York, NY 10011
www.hnabooks.com